Alfred's Premier Piano Express

Dennis Alexander, Gayle Kowalchyk, E. L. Lancaster, Victoria McArthur & Martha Mier

FOREWORD

Alfred's *Premier Piano Express Repertoire, Book 2* includes motivational music in a variety of styles, reinforcing concepts introduced in *Premier Piano Express, Book 2*. The pieces (including one duet) in this book correlate page by page with the materials in *Premier Piano Express*. They should be assigned according to the instructions in the upper-right corner of each page of the book.

All music was composed or arranged by Dennis Alexander and Martha Mier. The music in this book can be used as supplementary repertoire for any method. Students will enjoy performing these pieces for family and friends in a formal recital or on special occasions.

ONLINE ACCESS INCLUDED

🔊 Audio Performances and Orchestrated Accompaniments

TNT² Practice Software

To access the audio and software, visit:
alfred.com/redeem

Enter this code:
00-48631_228822

CONTENTS

ISBN-10: 1-4706-4341-3
ISBN-13: 978-1-4706-4341-6

Alfred Music
P.O. Box 10003
Van Nuys, CA 91410-0003
alfred.com

Cover Images:
Piano photo courtesy of Yamaha Corporation • Stack of paper image © Getty Images

Use with Premier Piano Express, Book 2, Unit 1, pages 8–9.

Saturday Blues  1

Dennis Alexander
Martha Mier

Moderately fast

A little slower

Press damper pedal and hold to end.

Use with Unit 2, pages 12–13.

Boogie Bounce 🔊 2

Dennis Alexander
Martha Mier

Press damper pedal and hold to end.

Shadows 🔊3

Dennis Alexander
Martha Mier

Mysteriously

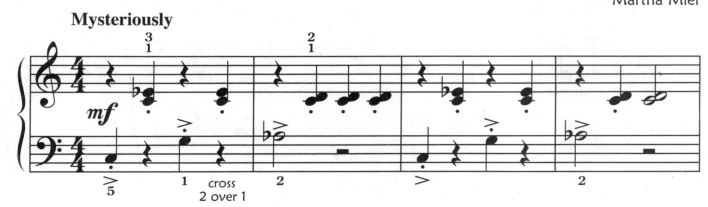

cross
2 over 1

✳ Lowest C
 • on piano
3

Use with Unit 3, page 19.

My Moonbeam 🔊 4

Dennis Alexander
Martha Mier

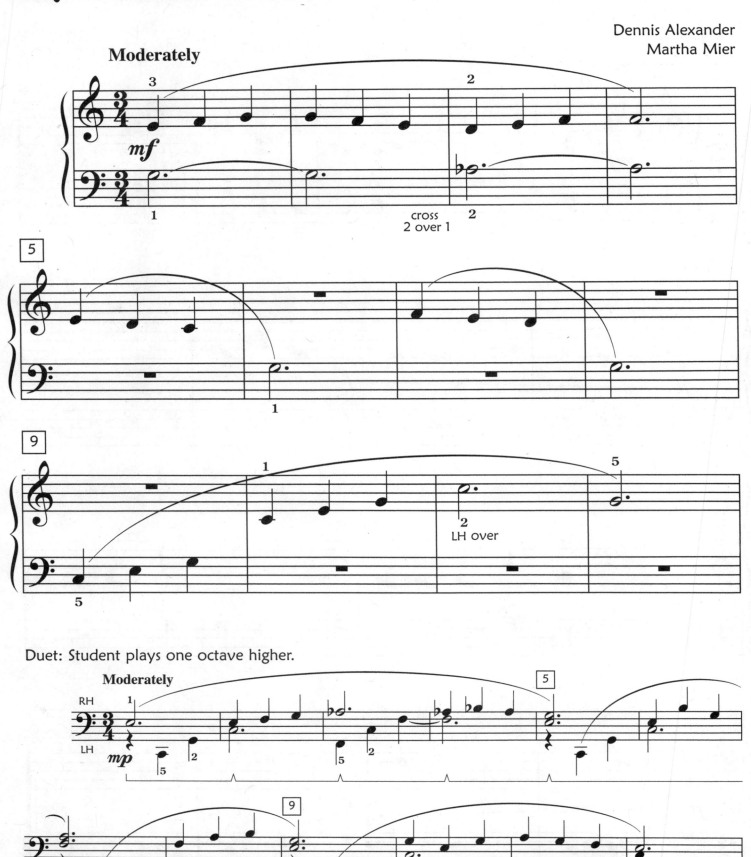

Duet: Student plays one octave higher.

Use with Unit 5, pages 24–25.

Together 🔊 5

Dennis Alexander
Martha Mier

Duet: Student plays one octave higher.

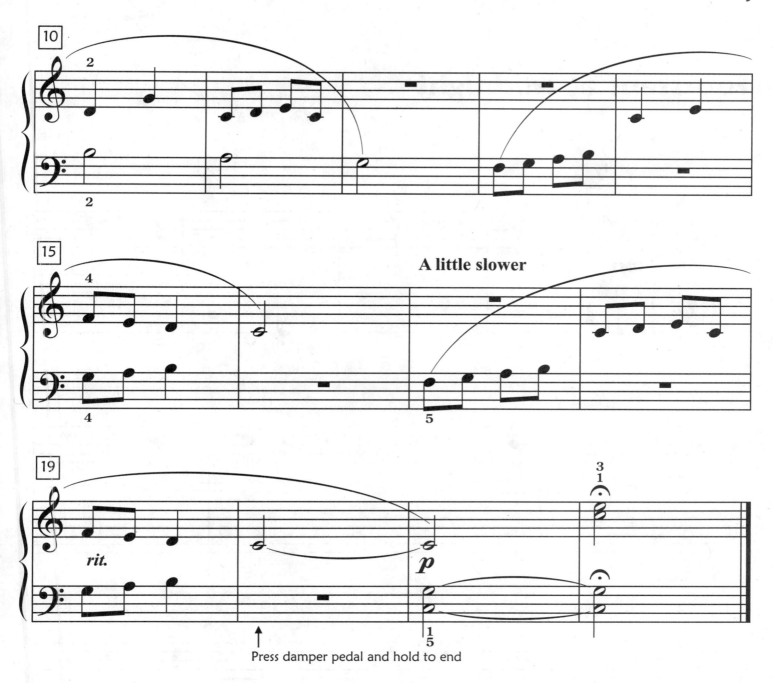

Press damper pedal and hold to end

Use with Unit 5, page 32.

Footsteps at Midnight

Dennis Alexander
Martha Mier

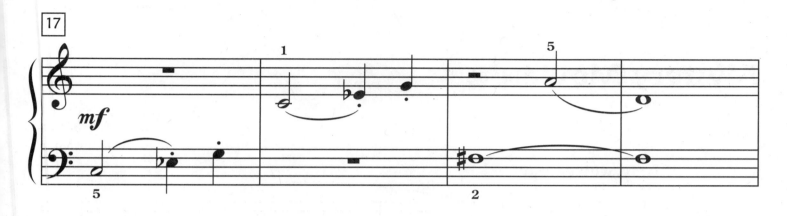

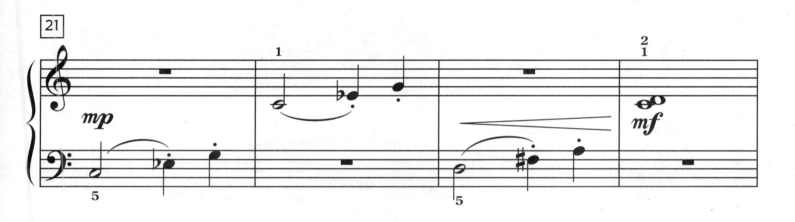

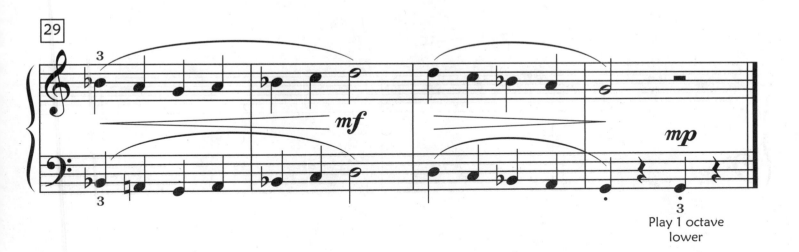

Play 1 octave
lower

Use with Unit 5, pages 36–37.

Mystery Movie

Dennis Alexander
Martha Mier

Lively, with energy

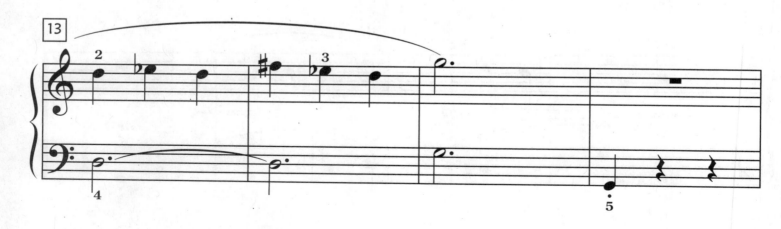

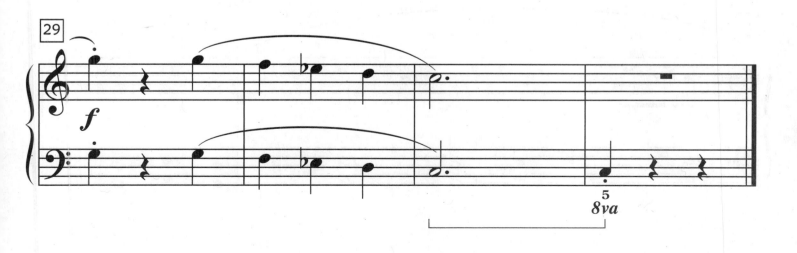

Use with Unit 6, page 40.

Desert Gold

Dennis Alexander
Martha Mier

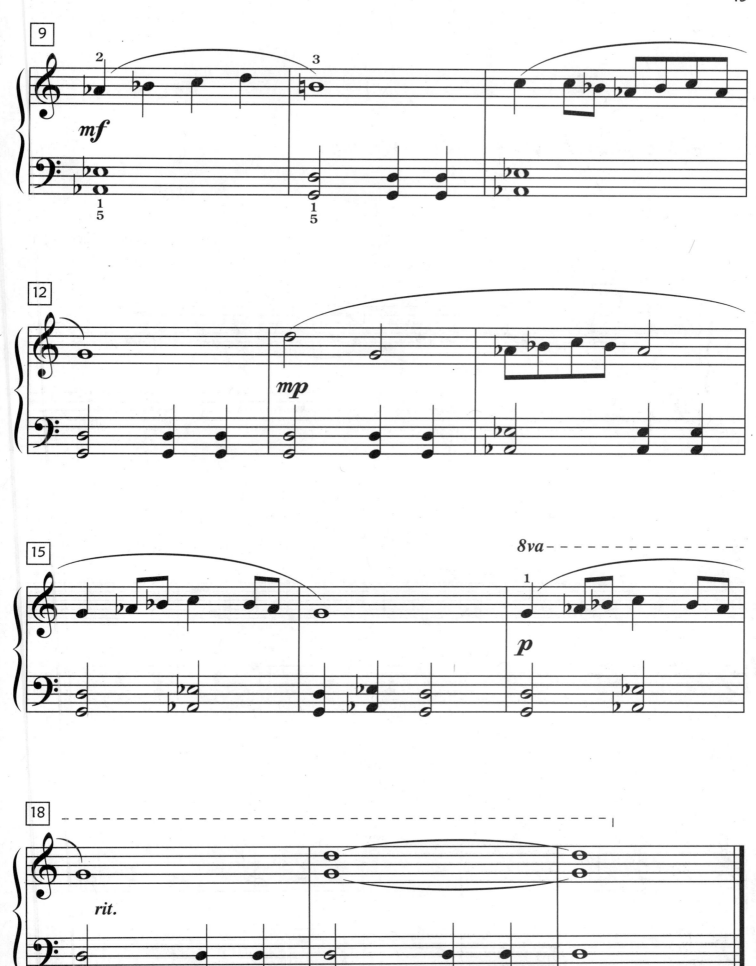

Use with Unit 7, pages 46–47.

The Answering Machine 🔊8

Dennis Alexander
Martha Mier

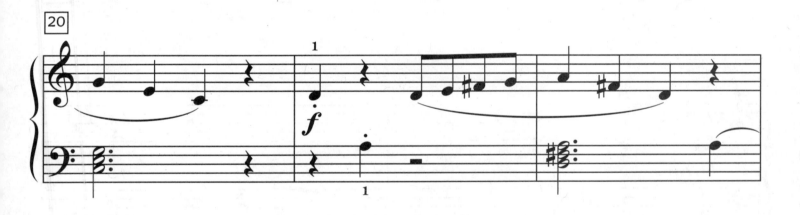

Use with Unit 8, pages 50–51.

Runaway Stagecoach 🔊9

Dennis Alexander
Martha Mier

To end this piece,
repeat the first page.

Use with Unit 8, pages 52–53.

Reach for the Stars

Dennis Alexander
Martha Mier

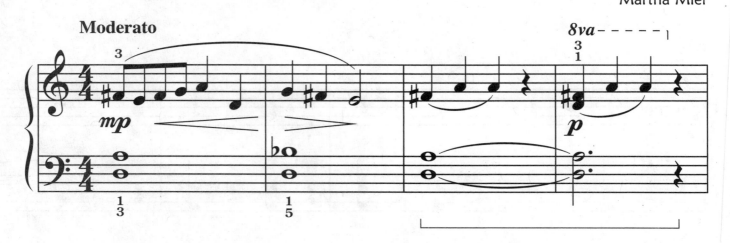

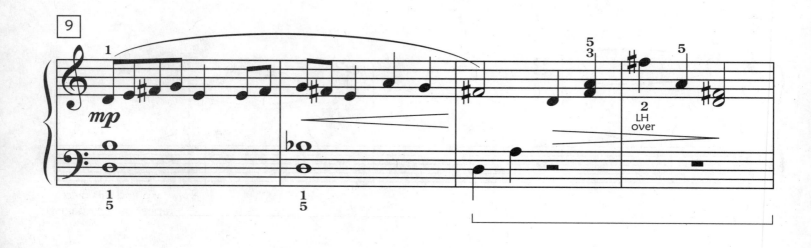

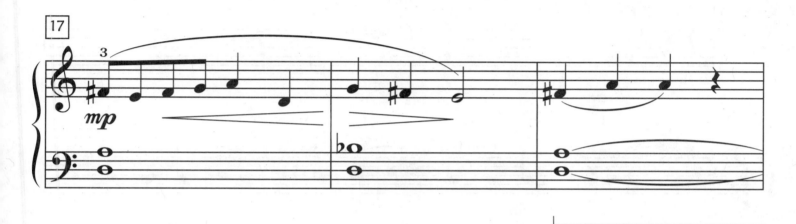

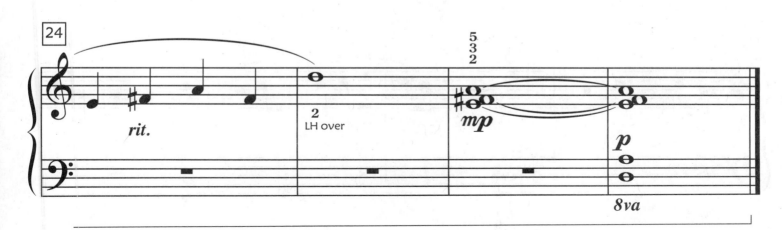

Use with Unit 9, pages 56–57.

Treasure Island 🔊10

Dennis Alexander
Martha Mier

Boldly, with spirit

Boldly, with spirit

Use with Unit 10, page 60.

Pirates at Sea

Dennis Alexander
Martha Mier

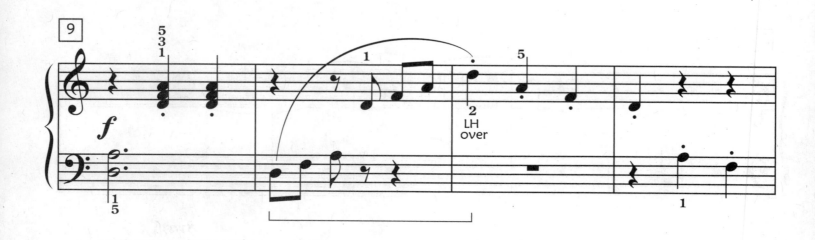

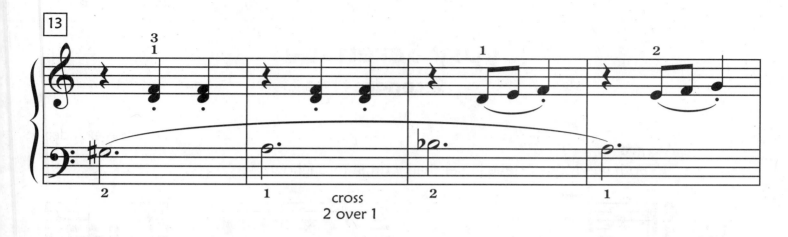

cross
2 over 1

Use with Unit 10, page 67.

Gypsy Serenade
Secondo

Dennis Alexander

Allegro
Both hands one octave lower than written throughout

Use with Unit 10, page 67.

Gypsy Serenade
Primo

Dennis Alexander

Allegro

Both hands one octave higher than written throughout

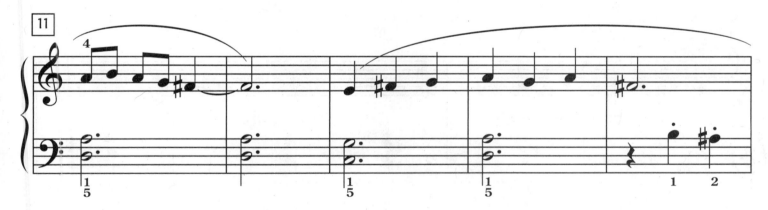

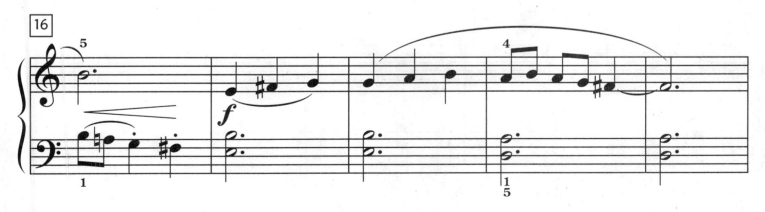

Secondo

Use with Unit 11, page 73.

A Cool Waltz 🔊 12

Dennis Alexander
Martha Mier

Moderate waltz tempo

Use with Unit 11, pages 74–75.

Royal Wedding

Dennis Alexander
Martha Mier

Joyfully, with celebration

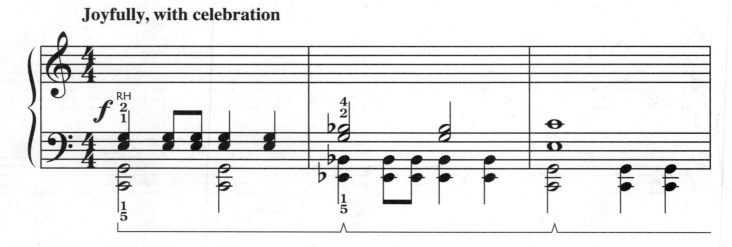

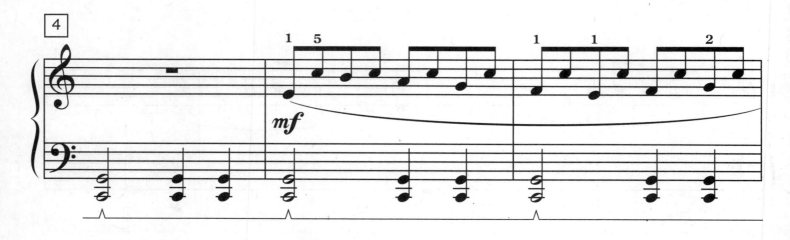

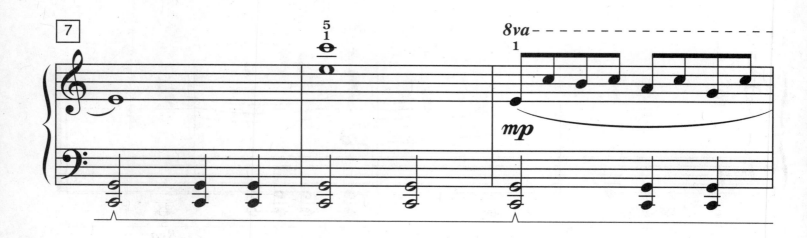

Use with Unit 12, pages 88–89.

Regal Dance 🔊 13

Dennis Alexander
Martha Mier

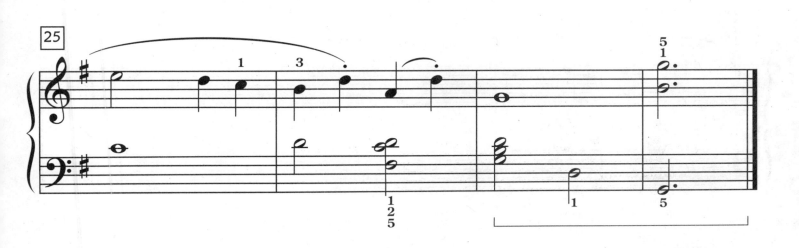

Use with Unit 13, page 92.

Inspector Beauregard 🔊 14

Dennis Alexander
Martha Mier

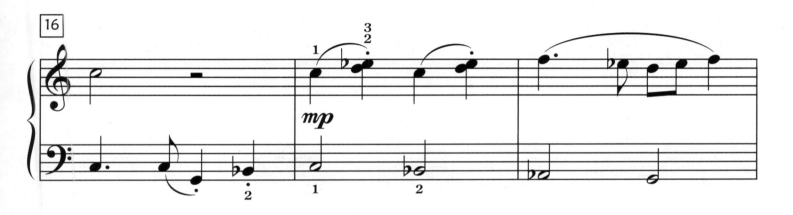

Use with Unit 13, pages 94–95.

Lemon Drop Rag  15

Dennis Alexander
Martha Mier

Moderato

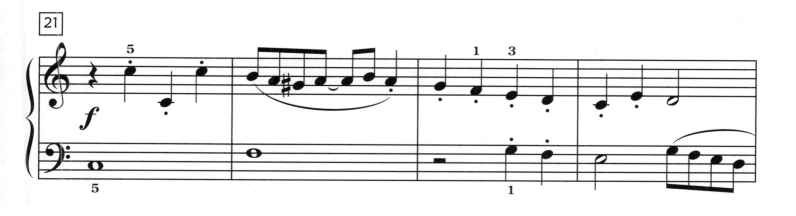

Audio Performances and Accompaniments

Stream or download audio performances on acoustic piano and orchestrated accompaniments for selected pieces in the book. Identified by a speaker icon (🔊) with a track number next to the title in the book, each selected piece includes four versions of audio:

- An acoustic piano performance at **performance tempo**.

- An acoustic piano performance at **practice tempo**.

- A digitally orchestrated accompaniment **with** piano.

- A digitally orchestrated accompaniment **without** piano.

Practice Software

For a more versatile practice experience, download the TNT 2 practice software, which allows the user to adjust the tempo of each track. Check the included Read-Me file for system requirements and installation instructions.